BLUE LASH

Also by James Armstrong
Monument in a Summer Hat

BLUE LASH

JAMES ARMSTRONG

MILKWEED EDITIONS

Published 2006 by Milkweed Editions
Cover design by Percolator
Cover photo by George Hoeylaerts/iStockphoto
Author photo by Dave Curl
Interior design by Percolator
The text of this book is set in ITC Stone Serif.
21 22 23 24 25 8 7 6 5 4

Milkweed Editions, a nonprofit publisher, gratefully acknowledges sustaining support from Emilie and Henry Buchwald; Bush Foundation; Patrick and Aimee Butler Family Foundation; Cargill Value Investment; Timothy and Tara Clark Family Charitable Fund; Dougherty Family Foundation; Ecolab Foundation; General Mills Foundation; Greystone Foundation; Institute for Scholarship in the Liberal Arts, College of Arts and Sciences, University of Notre Dame; Constance B. Kunin; Marshall Field's Gives; McKnight Foundation; a grant from the Minnesota State Arts Board, through an appropriation by the Minnesota State Legislature, a grant from the National Endowment for the Arts, and private funders; an award from the National Endowment for the Arts, which believes that a great nation deserves great art; Navarre Corporation; Debbie Reynolds; St. Paul Travelers Foundation; Ellen and Sheldon Sturgis; Target Foundation; Gertrude Sexton Thompson Charitable Trust (George R. A. Johnson, Trustee); James R. Thorpe Foundation; Toro Foundation; Serene and Christopher Warren; W. M. Foundation; and Xcel Energy Foundation.

Library of Congress Cataloging-in-Publication Data

Armstrong, James, Ph. D.
Blue lash / James Armstrong.—1st ed.
    p. cm.
ISBN-13: 978-1-57131-424-6 (pbk. : alk. paper)
ISBN-10: 1-57131-424-5 (pbk. : alk. paper)
1. Superior, Lake, Region—Poetry. I. Title.
PS3551.R4676B58 2006
811'.54—dc22
                              2005027356

For my parents, Bill and Ellen Armstrong

BLUE LASH

NORTH OF DULUTH

ISLE ROYALE

SOUTH SHORE

Properly speaking, there is no longer any world, there are only fragments of a shattered universe, an amorphous mass consisting of an infinite number of more or less neutral places in which man moves, governed and driven by the obligations of existence incorporated into an industrial society.

—Mircea Eliade, *The Sacred and the Profane*

BLUE LASH

NORTH OF DULUTH

UNQUENCHABLE ONTOLOGICAL THIRST

We long for pure water—
the blue that looks through us
because we are bottomless—
we long for the wave's shout of anger
on the old coast of abandoned fires.
We long for the Tyrian purples of the headland
and the torn white banners of the north wind
because our days are without a center—
we go on like a damaged propeller
cavitating in the foam.

THREE CROW SONGS

1.

The crows are on the road everywhere
like Bulgarian policemen;
they shrug their shoulders
then turn their backs to you—
one is inspecting this sun-dried carcass
with a bobbing cheerful purposefulness,
pecking at the leather edges,
as if to say *What have we here?*
Well, well. We can make something of this.
They are objective, observant,
not at all partisan,
cheerfully indifferent to suffering.
Your suffering, that is.

2.

I have a crow feather,
picked up from the roadside—
it's not as black as it's painted
but smoke gray, with waves
smooth and monotonous
like the lines in an engraving
in the *Police Gazette:*
even the devil's habits
are kind of repetitive.
Why light as a feather?
Because it's hollow,
a little drinking straw
with its barbels swept back
in a rockabilly haircut.

3.
All day one crow has been rowing
his creaky oars
up and down the shore road.
The sun flashes in his underwings
with the gleam of hair oil
worn by a long-ago scoutmaster
who liked to start campfires with gasoline.
A minute ago, he was
beaking the wet intestines
of a duck, dead on the median—
now he is soaring above a fir tree,
looking for baby starlings.
His flight is melodramatic gesticulation,
his black gloves extended
as if to say *abracadabra*—
he lands on a little branch end
of a poplar,
bobbing like a cork.
Whatever crime he is up to,
he forgives himself.

BASALT OUTCROP

It rests on one pained hip,
tilted vertiginously
toward the Pleistocene,
its face immobile and seamed.
The sun warms it, gently.
All up and down the beach are the
storm-rounded fragments
of its heyday.
It keeps its broken face to the sun,
a lizard basking,
oblivious to the harebell's
teenage makeup.

But in one dark cleft,
a spiderweb is trembling
in and out of daylight.

GABBRO

Oblong of stone,
sleek, voluptuous,
feminine,
heavy in my hand
as a weapon,
heavy as a storm wave,
gray as the storm,
lead-heavy, gull-gray,
you are neither all husk,
nor all interior,
your surface merely
the place where
content stops.
Mute as a thumb,
blind and orthodox,
rough to the touch
as a cat's tongue
but not without nuance—
under the glare of the sun
your crystals faintly glitter
like distant lakes
in the suburbs
of the underworld.

ORANGE LICHEN

Here on the beach, beside this barren lake,
I'm reading a book with my back to a ledge
which has been disinfected by a glacier.

Life cannot everywhere triumph
if we want to be alone.

But orange lichen is splashed
all over the boulders—
close up, the petalled structure
expands from the center
like suburbs or cancer, the optimism
of an organism
bent on wringing the silence
from each stone.

You find it wherever you look—
the intrepid virus, the pioneering bacterium,
breeding in deep sea vents, in the viscous darkness
of oil wells, on glaciers,
in the arid valleys of Antarctica.
Yet once raised to the level of humankind,
this cleverness turns suicidal, manic,
cutting the throats of children,
inventing the car bomb.

How peaceful
to be the only figure in a wilderness
as the wind rifles the pages of my book.
Here where the gulls cannot ask
for answers, where
I might retire
and translate death's blue sutras
into the vulgar language
of my era.

LUTHERAN SEA

One wave follows another
beneath the heel of the wind;
the spray blows landward,
but lacking salt or iodine
it smells oddly Protestant,
carrying the faintest tang
of wet iron,
well water
sluiced in a bucket
from a cabin you visited once
when you were a boy,
water that numbed the tongue
as if it had dripped
from a seam of ice,
blue and glistening,
in a cave
where nymphs of winter
with red fingers
preened before mirrors of frost,
dead cold sober.

TRAFFIC

All day long the great freighters
drive against the wind, breaking
blue water across their knees.
Gulls scream at the carnage.
The lake flutters its
white flags of surrender.
Then the wind dies down.
The shore grows indistinct.
The surf declines to a heaving mirror.
A few lights twinkle on,
coy and distant.
The ships pass the harbor light,
down-bound for Cleveland,
but seem to lose their narrative.
The lake beckons them in
under the night's dark columns.
The phosphorescent wake
beneath each heavy prow
trembles, like
fingers unbuttoning
a thin silk blouse.

CASTAWAYS

The storm waves banged all night—
an insane percussion section.
Now the beach seems garish,
crowded with castoffs. It's
a museum of the orphaned and abandoned,
the Kwik Trip of preforms,
the junkshop of stones.
My boots clack along the strand,
stirring up quartz eyes
hazed with glaucoma,
chipped flywheels, miniballs,
stone bearings gone out of round,
ossified cough lozenges,
keepsake lockets
clenching their cameos
like recalcitrant oysters,
basalt pralines,
stone-age coasters
and stove lids,
rounded granite skulls
each seeking a Hamlet
amidst the backwash.
Here's a piece of angle iron,
pounded to abstraction;
here, a plastic bobber
in scarlet high-water pants,
like Fatty Arbuckle.

I think of my grandfather's
workshop bench—
the Folgers cans full of
screws in odd sizes,
wing nuts and rusted bolts,
hinges nostalgic for doors.

Here is a birch log
drying out several feet inland.
All night it sailed,
flapping its ghostly parchment.

When we find the other scroll,
we'll have the whole testament.

DULUTH

It's a city like a shabby amphitheater
where the lake does summer stock
among old granaries and ore docks:
dinner theater, romantic comedies,
dance numbers out of *Captain January*.
The big ships lurk like Homeric props:
like the lobster traps
in a Midwestern fish restaurant.

But winter is highbrow: marathon
stagings of Strindberg and Beckett,
obscure operas in the minimalist mode,
the bare proscenium extending to the horizon,
the chorus in white robes,
the north wind singing the same note over and over
until the ticket holders
want to go home
and kill themselves.

LEFT BEHIND

Blue shadows race
over the damp cobbles
of a wide deserted beach
littered with cans
of Old Milwaukee Lite—
spent cartridges
from a twenty-four-gun salute.
A lingering, sickly incense
rises from the
crumpled glitter
beside the driftwood logs
and cigarette butts.

And wouldn't you take this cheap
transcendence, over the
alternative?

Above the supine horizon
of work and more work,
the vertical threatens
like a thundercloud.
It mounts and mounts
until something must happen—
the rifle-crack,
then the downpour.
You're wet to the skin,
shivering, reborn,
under the wheeling weather—
you abandon your past self,
your lighter,
your navy blue sweater.

LINES CULLED FROM PETRARCH

The blue beard of twilight, the skies threatening rain—
the few notes of the white-throated sparrow,
the lonely spill of lake water in the wilderness;
the tick of the clock, the *om* of the refrigerator.
For one week, and a view of this inland ocean,
I've traveled north, turned the clock back on spring,
knelt at the altar light of the shadbush
and heard the nesting warbler's plaintive flute.
But you aren't here to share these silences
or my cabin, with its crates of books,
or my window, in whose proscenium
the lake turns violet. Yet
you are so slender, here is room for your absence;
one person in the world worth being alone with.

KENTUCKY WONDERS

I'm thinking about your
coiled hose and muddy trowel.
You like the way the bean sprouts lift
their swan necks above the crumbled soil,
the way the squash blossoms
open their saffron cotillions.
It's like the way, when you talk to horses
their ears swivel, delicate periscopes,
and their humid gaze turns in your direction.
So much power, welded to gentleness,
so much gentleness, wedded to power—
little insistent threads of seedlings
a single frost might blacken.
By midsummer, they are a solid wall.

A WEEK AWAY

I uncurl the wire clasps on the
bag of coffee you bought me:
inside, the aroma of earth,
edible and fragrant.
Two spoonfuls into the filter,
a gout of hot water,
and the sky will take one giant step
closer. I think of
how you slid these black beans
from the dispenser,
so they felt like bees in a sack;
how you poured them into the grinder
which rumbled like my grandfather's
old electric turn-stone
on which he would lean
a knife's edge, and make it spark
with all he was taking away;
how I am sharpening my heart
now, on the grit of your absence,
laying it on the whirling surface
of the day, until
I can feel it grow incandescent,
trailing the hair of a comet, as
whatever does not love you streaks away.

PURL

The slap and take-up,
the little jig
of ice water over gravel—
lace and bauble
and ripple—
each stone like the nose
of a seal,
or a moistened lip—
density's
ache and rebuff,
love's
divided kingdoms
that meet
by caress
and incursion.

BEACHED GAS BOAT

(Stoney Point, Duluth)

The engine squats amidships,
sprouting cracked wires. The rusted bolts of the manifold
are screwed down on silence,
all gauges zeroed.
On the canted hull,
the paint is reptilian; thick
yellow chips give off their ancient perfume
of turpentine. The bilge is green with algae
on pools of rainwater.
Under the decking the thick wrist of the driveshaft
follows the keel to nowhere—
to the green rose of the propeller.
On the stern plate, the iron bar of the tiller
is jammed hard over.

PROTO

Certain stones are older than all records—
from a time before thumbprints or bacteria,
when the earth was someplace quiet,

all angels and no television.
Thousands of years went by, and no one counted them,
the annals of fire and steam

before protozoa, before the airplane,
before the poet
whose bones are eternal

but whose flesh is grass and
ripe for the mower:
where he's going predates them, and the moon.

Scout around the bays. Each has been scraped clean
with the shoulder blade of a mastodon.
The continent sheds its sediment

and becomes the wreck that dreams are made of:
the lake approves it. All that blue in motion.
The mirror flashes in the wave's cup.

QUARTZ PEBBLE

As a boy, reaching under
the lake's nightgown,
how often I would seize you,

little knuckle,
petrified egg,
white as a wave cap,

far on the horizon,
gull wing against storm-wrack:
little crack in the varnish

where the canvas shows through.
Wet, you are searching and lucent—
dry, mere chalk.

If Melville doesn't mention you
in his chapter on pallor,
it's only because to hold you

is to grow more intimate
with seams and lodes,
shadow organs. Now

you want to talk,
you want to disclose
(I hold you up to the light)

the blood clot
of your heart.

MAY

The lake is calm now, and laps the rocks,
a cat cleaning its paws
while the morning sun hangs her damp laundry.

I'm squatting on warm stones
watching three loons
jostle each other for fish,

dipping their sleek heads
under the seal-
gray swell.

A word comes to my tongue:
it's smooth, like a drupe of beach glass
in the shallows,

green as an aphid among hard pebbles.
The lake mouthed it once—
the lake mouths everything.

Every stone was once an argument.
In the end, each fits with the next
as though it were joined and sanded,

pieced into a mechanism
with which we might manufacture a better world.
But it is neither gear

nor shard,
the word I'm thinking of.
It isn't force.

It isn't even love.

EREMITE

We do not love life the way we say we do:
life moves from strength to frailty, from frailty to dust.
Instead we trust the gray inanimate

stone that does not move,
the stars that move unchangingly.
I love this violent blue

lake that beats the black shore with its fists
and withdraws with a bony clack.
I would rather lie down among monuments

no one remembers,
these hills of humpback stone
over which the birches

raise their paper crosses,
while the gull shrills, the wide-winged
dove of hunger—

I would rather walk the thin-lipped shore
the way saints do their alkaline deserts,
as if each stone were the key to paradise.

CATECHISM

What's under you?
Layers of inhuman heartache, the butterfly strata,
the earth's skull, spent javelins of the sun,
white bones standing in line for scripture
and turning to history:
the basement that understands us,
on which the world pours
the unction of its tears
until they become a fragile mirror
which moves with the breath of the wind.

PRAYER

If we don't believe in heaven, who reads the letters we mail there
    every evening?
Children send most of them, kneeling by the bedpost
imagining the universe under the care of a father
who rumbles behind the newspaper
smelling of cigarettes and Old Spice.
To grow up is to lose one's God at sea—
better to lose one than be one.
If you believe the world is perfect,
think of Keats dying young.
I never would have seen it if I hadn't believed it,
the saying goes. Somebody has to awaken us
to the time of day it is when the earth is empty
of any intention, or any human presence.

And yet it is noon, and here you are—your blue headlands
and swords, your wave-moistened silences.
As if at the heart of things
there were a heart.

BELLA DONNA

The cicadas grind their teeth
under the blue roof of August,
the heat places its heavy hand on the landscape,
but you never flinch.
One breath from you
and the birches shiver,
The beach rose closes up shop midday;
a white fog hides the dock, like the faded sheets
thrown over furniture in the great house
when the mistress goes abroad.
In sudden October,
boats rub their moorings
like horses in a stall
and even the gulls look thoughtful.

Later you grant everyone a reprieve.
The sun casts off its cover, a
glare returns to the dock.
But you glitter restlessly, back and forth
out every window.
Your smile has the iron look
of one who's certain of her vast removal.

AUBADE

The sky is still and blue-white
over the lake's roughed-up gray
of little chop—on the horizon,
the powder blue eyelid of Wisconsin
is not yet open.
A red-eyed vireo
announces the self's old claim in the birches:
Here I am. Look at me.
I need a girlfriend.
Now the field sparrow starts up
his song like a spun dime,
and the ovenbird, demanding
teach me, teach me.
Rain will fall
on the lake's satin slacks,
on the whalebacks of porphyrite,
but I won't be here to see it.
Good-bye, Cabin Seven, my
rented Walden, my
cockpit hermitage,
where I threshed out the old
lover's quarrel with language.
Good-bye, lake,
restless basin of sibilants,
you who keep the climate cool
and wet the mind's appetite
for transcendence.

SEPTEMBER

I miss the tilt and racket of your face,
the collapsing factories of your anger,
the shoreline wearing your boas of foam—
the steel mirror of your silence,
your glass contingencies, in the night's hold.
I miss the morning's coverlet of cloud,
one gull flying east over the moving distances
while closer in
the same boulder is kissed again and again.
As the blacksmith plunges the bruised steel into the tub,
erasing the heat of his industry,
I have cooled my brow
with the ice of your disdain—
I have held your cold hand in the rain.

ISLE ROYALE

CABIN PASTORAL

Each morning the light crept in
unheralded, caught us sleeping
unlocked, unused to a silence

that wasn't silent except in our sense,
as the wave and stone made a loud business
of mutual annihilation.

In fact, the merganser whose wings
whistled overhead on her descending
flight path, toward her bay-fishing

sisters, *she* thought the north wind
was loud and drowned the cries of her ducklings
on flat cove-water, in care of the thin

unmated female—another sibling?
Or aunt? A widow?
The herring gull's yellow eye

was sharp for morsels.
All are watchful. Delving and businessing
is what nature does

harshly and best. As for us,
whose only employment
was to weigh each day in the balance,

we were under the sign of the moose
whose prongs were nailed
above our front entrance,

bitten by mice and frost—
splendid and cryptic,
like outdated equipment.

SCHEDULED STOP

(from an early photograph of Isle Royale)

Ice block and sawdust breathe the vapor of winter
on crates of gutted lake trout bound for Chicago
with northern tinfoil caught in their wide-open eyes.
Having just loaded them, three fishermen in coveralls
lean on the pilings, knitting their Sabbath.
The steamship's prow is an axe edge of cream,
a sheet of foolscap on which is painted
the word *AMERICA*. Under coal smoke it comes,
under the black top hat: it is the
delicate iron of civilization.
Fifteen feet up, at the railing, the tourists
in neckties and sport coats—gawkers,
readers of Ruskin or *Walden,* the
women in mutton sleeves and exogamous hats—
look down on the wilderness. The
island's fir-tipped war bonnet
bristles like a painted backdrop.

TENTING

(Scoville Point, Isle Royale, 1904)

It is a bivouac of women
in placketed shirtwaists and ankle-length skirts,
hair up in pins, each
perched on the downed birch log,
hands folded respectfully.
Father sits behind them, a little blurry:
the old juridical owl, in post-bellum whiskers,
giving the photographer his "summon the bailiff" look.
He wants his coffee,
and you can see it there, at the photo's center,
the little vessel of tinware
on top of the cook pans and crates of supplies.
Who'll light the fire? Who'll take care of him?
The women think of their freedom
under the dining fly.
The lake wind ruffles the thick folds of their skirts.
The forest is a house without walls.

THE EDISON FISHERY

(from a painting by Richard Schilling)

The warped strakes of the gas boats in their cradles
on the cobbles, canted at empty angles,
are someone's text or testament, open to weather
with August's daisies for audience.
What the fishermen had to speak of, they kept to themselves;
what they believed was paid out, or hauled in, or knotted
by lamplight. That this would outlast their efforts
they didn't think—the shoals were heaped with damage
after the storm-pummel, the abandoned outfit
battered to driftwood on the ledges.
The fish swim somewhere else,
but these have been kept from all effort—
each dry plank wants out, and worries its nail;
in the hold, you can see daylight.

SCOVILLE POINT FLOW

I'm sluicing the greasy flatware and handling
the camp mugs with rubber gloves, thinking
of Keats's cold hermit above a human shore—
his metaphor for the star
which kindles now among the shaking poplar leaves
out this window, steadfast as the day-blush
wanes. I know where a warbler stirs on her cup
of needles and tinder, packthread and birch fluff;
she is small and dutiful enough.
I know where a merganser fishes late in the inlet
and pecks diffidently at an inverted moon—
but the evening will not be domestic.
The pink museum of the fireweed is closing up;
they are locking the exhibits.

GEOLOGY

All day, all day, I have been reading:
porphyrite, traprock, felsite, rose
quartz and prehnite, the uplift of sequences,
subsidence, dip and anti-dip, crazy fractures—
seams of red fire; then the matriarchal on-slosh,
the era of bony fishes and nonbony fishes,
horsetail rushes and proto-crocodiles;
above silted-up bays, the pulsing wings
of a Carboniferous dragonfly—
then the clean break.
The great block-plow of the glacier
glittering, edging and backing, leaving the world-ribs
flensed and glistening,
a wilderness of blue gravel and braided outflow.

CANADIAN BROADCAST

I was twenty-five when I first came into this
secular light, and its astringent cleanliness:
away with the old idols, their quaint shadows,
the fear in earnest faces. Away with
the Revised Standard Bible, the banged drum
of progress, the notion of human hope.
Now the portable radio beside the sink is playing
a Bach piece. It's sad and formal
and I have a vision of the composer's kind disappointment,
his face bending over the lined sheet, with all its little notes—
I can see how the longing for order is always predicting
his work, but never consoling him,
though we are consoled.
For a moment we are consoled.

CONSTELLATIONS

Is there a religious happiness
in the twilight that deepens beyond the inlet,
that infinite picture,
the border of dark on dark?
The pewter stars are faded and childlike
in the day's mausoleum, but night brings them out
on schedule. The sun merely glanced at them—
the night knows better, knows there is an order
in looking at one thing after another:
an act that connects, so we can't think of them after
except as figures, as furniture, as childhood's Monopoly tokens
grown mythically larger:
The boot, the ship, the car.
The harp, the cup, the crown.

EMERSON ISLAND

A handful of harebells, a
swale of flowering mint, one
nesting warbler, two or three bees
bumbling among the white angles of
four birch trees,
and the fragrant spear point
of a balsam.
Of the original inhabitants: a few scraps of tin,
a collapsed foundation
flagged with fireweed.
Some relative of Ralph Waldo Emerson
made his personal pact with nature here:
now he is gone, and
nature carries on without him.
Algae thickens the cribs
of his ruined dock—
deep in green water,
a school of fish
noses his privilege.

SOUTH SHORE

There is intemperance in nature, in the terrific force of storms, in the immensity of the sands, in glaciers and snow-capped peaks, in the exuberance of vegetal and animal life, in the excesses of the human masses in agitation.

—Alain, "The Great Mysteries"

INVECTIVE

Sunset opens her cabinets of rose—
a loon flies out of a drawer,
draping her shivering note
on the black pine tops
as an inbound jet ski
revs past the dock
like a demon out of Milton,
the driver bent over his handlebars
seeing nothing
but where he is going.
He carries my happiness off
under his arm;
his wake hisses on the rocks
like the serpents
of Pandemonium.

So I curse him: May he
live in the boiler room of purgatory
with a car alarm wired around his neck
and a weed-whacker up his ass.
May he be reborn as the last shovelful of gravel
in a county dump truck
traveling a corduroy road,
or a bit of grit in a cracked piston, or
a beer can full of yellow jackets
propped up for target practice.

May he be strapped naked
to the muffler of a Harley-Davidson
ridden by an obese black-leather angel
into the brown heat-haze of the city.

May he realize the hell
he has been made prince of.

FLOTSAM AND JETSAM

The morning beach is draped with detritus
in a sinuous conga line—delicate
cedar roots,
fir cones, alder leaves,
stray bits of driftwood
whose smooth hydraulic shapes
look like car hoods from the '30s,
scrolls of birch bark
carry the news
from moose to moose—
a few pale cigarette filters,
a stray flap of Mylar (somebody's
birthday balloon, once),
a crayfish claw,
moustaches of brown foam.
These were flotsam,
but they didn't drown—
they're drying out on the sand,
like Crusoe, or Jonah.

But the blue S of this dead heron
with his head in the foam,
his articulate stilts
run aground
so the small clear surf
pushes his accordion neck
back and forth, his yellow beak
drilling at cold nothing—
is he ashore or afloat?
His feet are on dry land,

his head in the trough of a wave,
caught between dry dock
and dream.

THE THREE SISTERS

Shipwrecks offer their axioms
plucked from the boiling lake
as the dripping stern disappears
and the ship's name, in white letters—
the *Aurelia*, or the *Philo P. Lawson*,
or the *City of Ontonagon*—
grows dimmer and dimmer
behind the lake's blue curtain:
Don't take voyages in late November,
don't go out of port if you dream
you're choking on ice water or see
the floating O of a life preserver
washing ashore on the beach
at Whitefish Point.
Don't set out to sea despite the weather,
making one last run to Cleveland—
ride out the storm in safe harbor.
The lake gods punish heedlessness,
they don't respect shipping schedules.
Most of all, say the old narratives,
beware of the Three Sisters,
wave-daughters of the nor'easter:
one pummels the bow with a
turquoise hammer—another
tosses you on your beam ends
and before your boat can shrug off the
deckful of angry lake water,
the third one crests:
perhaps you see her,
lit by storm lightning,

a titanic bride
in her veils of spray—
then she buries you
among the dark shapes of your cargo—
not as on dry land,
moored to the certainty
of a granite marker,
but anonymously,
among small avid mouths.

BLEAK HOUSE

The grass is steel wool under the swing set
and the walnut sheds leaves of anachronistic yellow;
the hosta are burnt as though with a welder's torch.
The canoe lies hull-up against the rusty fence,
a green tapered shape, inverted and idle.

I think of blue Superior,
noisy with all that water
and cold as a snowcone.
I think of the reams of data
in some NOAA conference room:
the average daily temperature,
the means and extremes.
I think of a parking lot
in Christmas, Michigan,
the trailers, with their powerboats and jet skis,
yoked to Yukons and Navigators
and Cherokees, shimmering in the heat: inside,
their owners, rampant for risk and
dissolution.

What have I done this summer?
Why have I shown my children
the secret cove, its glassy minuet?
The stage laugh of the loon?
The sough of wind in the pine crown?
Like Jarndyce in Dickens,
they will be hopeful while others
gamble away their inheritance,

throwing down what they cannot
afford to lose.

JET SKI

On the wooden balcony
overlooking the gaudy buttresses
of the Pictured Rocks, I can see them,
Day-Glo waterbugs
slapping pellucid shoal-water:
the roar is distant and quaint.
Their wake rocks the kayakers like a statement:
Get out of the way
of the insistent present.

The year I lived in West Rogers Park,
there was a billboard above the street
which through all four abrupt Chicago seasons
showed a giant couple riding a Ski-Doo
through a green wall of spray.
The edges of the photo were blurred
as though all matter were dissolving into excited particles.
The couple were taut-skinned and tan;
despite their sunglasses
you could see their elation,
their heads thrown back with the acceleration—
it was like an abduction out of Ovid,
sexy and thrilling.
Below them, pale men and women
waited in line for the bus.

It *is* something—to realize your desire
is chromium yellow and
ride it to the horizon,
to steer a god's chariot
roughshod over the limit.
It is like leaving the bar with a woman
who is not your wife,
or finding a wallet in the street,
or winning the LOTTO:
desire's sudden
gratuitous amplification.
It confirms our human need
not to be under the thumb
of the grim boss, necessity.
Even if we know
how a story like that must end.

The wave-riders circle
and head back to the dock.
Their wakes crisscross and dissipate
in the mortal glint of the lake.
Nothing remains of their ride
but the faint blue smoke
of their sacrifice,
rising upward.

THE BOILER

On Muskrat Point, a riveted drum
wets its ankles in the calm
like a fat lady bathing.
Hard to picture it as the original lung
of a donkey engine,
a purse of furious vapor
cranking a winch on a salvage boom—
wresting some sodden timber off the
dark lake bottom.
Now it's a curiosity,
forensic and rusty,
on which the gulls
sit and preen.

This is the same sand spit
where an Ojibwa war party
drank itself mad with trader's whiskey:
Three days of slurred singing,
firing muskets into the air.
Then silence.
The trader saw them through his spyglass
lying on the wide beach
as though dead.

Every spree runs aground eventually;
there are not enough spirits to float us
into paradise.
The sandbar itself is a
child of inebriation,
cast up by a drunken lake
which the east wind
lashed to idiot foam.

But what if a spree
defines a civilization?

It was a roaring night
that dragged this barrel of iron
out of the lake depths—
forged in some ironworks downstate
and cribbed in white oak,
then burst by the wave-paw
and rolled like a plaything.
Now the minnows flicker like confetti
in the sun-dappled shallows.
The boiler grows warm and empty
and red with rust.

Someone places a rock on its dented lid
like an afterthought.

THE WRECK
for Dot

In the calm of Murray Bay, the island inverts itself:
the brush-tips of pines reach into a wavering sky
through which the sand bottom gleams, as in double exposure.
Three times a day the tour boat crosses the harbor

to pause at the wreck-buoys over the *Bermuda*—
I can hear the megaphone, faintly, over the water.
Through the glass bottom, tourists look with interest
at drowned deck timbers, the green yawn of the hatchway.

Lake Superior: Graveyard of the Lakes
says the map we bought, labeled "historically correct."
On the lake's lupine silhouette, the little drawings of downed ships
cruise the black water: a flotilla of ghosts.

Sloop or ketch, whaleback, surf tug, lake freighter—
coffins in the damp, now; names to remember:
the *Colorado*, the *Sunbeam*, the *Samuel Foster*,
the *Harry Steinbrenner*, the *George M. Cox*, the *Prussia*,

the *South Shore*, the *Starruca*, *Kiowa*, and *Servia*,
the *Batchawanna*, the *Golspie* and the *Grace*—
testaments to the romance of disaster
and the exactitude of marine insurance.

You read them nonstop,
in paperbacks bought at the gift shop,
those tales, whose narratives always begin
in sunlight, in mild weather, the captain optimistic—

despite the heavy foreshadowing.
They work their way to the predictable end:
lifeboats overturned, the water boiling with objects,
propellers spinning incongruously in the air

as the ship begins her *long sleigh ride to the bottom.*
In every tale, the lake is the superb antagonist,
covetous, secretive, predatory.
Her numb embrace drags the unwary down:

a truer plot than our official optimism.
What the sea teaches, any sailor knows:
the world's appetite for us is unslakeable.
Our mistake is in thinking we can't drown.

But I can't explain why you've come to love it,
our nightly reading: *the ship was torn in half*
and sank in just eight minutes, with all hands.
Or: *Horrified we watched her burn to the waterline.*

Not for you, the rabbit salads of Beatrix Potter.
People were crying out among the wreckage,
and then there was only silence—
by the time the Coast Guard reached them, it was too late.

When we got back downstate,
you wanted a shipwreck party for your birthday.
Your friends sat on the carpet wearing life jackets
while I read stories about haunted lighthouses

and Flying Dutchmen. A video of the *Titanic*
hushed them: a series of still photographs
taken by sailors of the recovered dead,
their ashen, indrawn faces.

And then the cake: the hull of the HMS *Brittanic*
sculpted in buttercream, tinted a lurid blue
as though submerged fathoms down in the Adriatic.
You blew all eight candles out,

just beginning to know that without warning
the raked bow of the world looms out of the fog—
already the horizon urges you toward the voyage
we all take, from which none of us return.

OLD TOWN

Double-ended, elongate fin or pod,
borrowed from the Ojibwa without permission,
labial shape, airship of white rapids,
aboriginally held together
with gum and spruce root,
cousin of the basket—
we have the modern equivalent, in green Royalex plastic,
with lacquered gunnels and wicker seats,
bought with a credit card in Madison, Wisconsin,
one chilly day in the fall
when my younger daughter was just an infant—
a gift from my father-in-law,
for the camping family he hoped we'd become.
I drove home with the unfamiliar
Turkish slipper
lashed to the top of my car,
listening to deer-camp songs on the radio.

Now, bobbing in chill lake water
pushed by the flat-bladed paddle,
it pulses forward, like something in the blood.
Aboard, four lunch sacks,
four water bottles,
and all three of my darlings,
smelling of sun oil, on the lookout for loons
and an empty beach. We are held,
suspended, on these waters that I love—
cold and pure awhile yet—and our shadow
courses the lake bottom's sand ridges,
a dirigible over Arabia.

OLIGOTROPHIC

Dead. Cold. Clear
as air. Pure
as ice: it takes 180 years
for water to leave this basin,
which means—
says the limnologist on the radio—
if your nose were fine enough,
you could draw a cup and taste the musketry
of 1812, the ashes of Toronto.
The lake remembers more than we do:
Blood rinsed from a tomahawk,
carbon from the Cloquet fire,
iron ore in the bowels of the *Edmund Fitzgerald*,
the smell of Norwegian pancakes
from a cabin on the shore of Isle Royale in 1927;
the acrid taste of taconite,
the stink of bloated lake trout, stench of burning
pyramids of sturgeon. Potato peels
from Louis Agassiz's Harvard expedition
in 1845. The heel of a moccasin
awash in Two Harbors
in the McKinley administration.
The webbed feet of a fish duck
at the mouth of the Big Two-Hearted
River, right now, paddling.
A beer bottle tossed
from a party barge last night
in Murray Bay. Sawdust
from the last great white pines
of Grand Island

logged in the 1960s
and ferried across, section by section,
on this very lumber tug
tied to the dock
and leaking diesel.

ACKNOWLEDGMENTS

I would like to thank Orv Lund and Elizabeth Oness for their extremely helpful close readings of these poems in manuscript. I would also like to thank the members of my poetry group: Elle Newman, Gary Eddy, Linda Kukowski, Ken McCullough, and Judy Thorn, for their insights. Thanks are due to Louis Jenkins and Connie Wanek for encouragement and inspiration by example. I would also like to thank Janel Crooks of the Hiawatha National Forest for her support during my artist's residency on Grand Island. Thanks to Dave Curl for his unflagging support and encouragement. Thanks are also due to Mark and Kim Gilbertson of North Shore Cottages, where many of these poems were written. Finally, thanks to my wife, Laura, always my first and best reader and a fellow devotee of the Big Blue, and to my daughters Dot and Pippa.

These poems were made possible in part by grants from the Minnesota State Arts Board and the National Endowment for the Arts, as well as by residencies with Isle Royale National Park and Hiawatha National Forest.

I would like to thank the editors of the following publications, where these poems first appeared: "Scoville Point Flow"; "Geology"; "Canadian Broadcast"; and "Constellations" were published in *The Island Within Us*, published by the Isle Royale Natural History Association (2000). "Beached Gas Boat"; "September"; "Quartz Pebble"; "Proto"; "Cabin Pastoral"; "Scheduled Stop"; "May"; "Tenting"; "Eremite"; "Catechism"; "Prayer"; "The Edison Fishery" all appeared in different versions in *Purl*, a limited edition chapbook published by Syphon Press in 2003. "Proto"; "Eremite"; "May"; and "September" also were published as a small booklet accompanying the CD "The Mirror Flashes in the Wave's Cup," volume 4 of the *East of Eden* recorded poetry series produced by *Poetry East* (2002). "Tenting"; "Scheduled Stop"; "Inventory"; and "Proto" appeared in *Shade* Magazine (2006).

ABOUT THE AUTHOR

 When James Armstrong was thirteen years old, his family moved to Michigan from southern Indiana. They decided to drive up to the Upper Peninsula to take a look at the great inland sea at the top of the map. That was the beginning of a long love affair with Lake Superior.

After growing up in Kalamazoo, Michigan, Armstrong studied and taught in Boston and Chicago. His poems have appeared in *Triquarterly, Gulf Coast, Orion, The Snowy Egret, The New York Times Book Review, Shade,* and elsewhere. He has a PhD in American Literature from Boston University and has taught English and Creative Writing at Northwestern University and in the MFA program at the School of the Art Institute of Chicago. His book of poems *Monument in a Summer Hat* was published in 1999 by New Issues Press. A fine-arts press edition of his work on Lake Superior, entitled *Purl,* was published in May of 2003 by Syphon Press. Armstrong received the PEN-New England Discovery Prize for poetry in 1996, and he has been awarded both an Illinois Arts Council Fellowship in poetry and a Minnesota State Arts Board Fellowship in poetry. He was an artist in residence at Isle Royale in 1994. For the past five years Armstrong has been a professor of English at Winona State University in Winona, Minnesota, where he lives with his wife and two daughters.

MORE POETRY FROM MILKWEED EDITIONS

To order books or for more information, visit *milkweed.org*

TURNING OVER THE EARTH
Ralph Black

MORNING EARTH:
FIELD NOTES IN POETRY
John Caddy

THE PHOENIX GONE,
THE TERRACE EMPTY
Marilyn Chin

WU WEI
Tom Crawford

THE ART OF WRITING:
LU CHI'S WEN FU
Translated from the Chinese
by Sam Hamill

PLAYING THE BLACK PIANO
Bill Holm

GOOD HEART
Deborah Keenan

FURIA
Orlando Ricardo Menes

THE PORCELAIN APES OF
MOSES MENDELSSOHN
Jean Nordhaus

FIREKEEPER: SELECTED POEMS
Pattiann Rogers

SOME CHURCH
David Romtvedt

FOR MY FATHER, FALLING ASLEEP
AT SAINT MARY'S HOSPITAL
Dennis Sampson

ATLAS
Katrina Vandenberg

milkweed
editions

Founded as a nonprofit organization in 1980, Milkweed Editions is an independent publisher. Our mission is to identify, nurture and publish transformative literature, and build an engaged community around it.

milkweed.org

Interior design by Percolator
Typeset in ITC Stone Serif by
Percolator